The Perseverance Of Beauty

ALSO BY M. E. FORBES

I Am Who I Believe I Am
(Empowering Affirmations and Contemplations for Children)

THE PERSEVERANCE OF BEAUTY

POEMS

M. E. FORBES

© 2024, Text by M. E. Forbes

All rights reserved. Except for brief quotations in critical articles or reviews, no part of this book may be reproduced without prior written permission from the author: M. E. Forbes.

www.meforbes.com

First edition, published 2024

Cover photo and design by M. E. Forbes

For my daughter
with infinite love and gratitude.

Contents

Part One: The Perseverance Of Beauty 2

Oh, so That's Poetry 3

Spellbound 5

We Don't Die Here. 6

The Morning Caller 7

Fog 8

Brush Off the Frown 9

The Petite French Country 11

They Never Know You at All 12

Left 13

This is the Moment 14

Proudly Everything, ... 15

The Same House on Fire, ... 16

We Are The Unblinking Eyes 19

The Same Difference 20

Some Will Hate You 21

2020 Vision 23

The Fledglings 24

All I Had to Lose 25

Downhill from Everywhere 26

Whatever Happens Or Doesn't Happen 27

In the Moon's Platinum Glow, ... 29

Life After Life 30

Digging for Plump Beetle Babies 31

In a Hammered Red Admiral's Dream, ... 32

The Plea	33
The Giants Are Afraid	34
I Keep Forgetting	35
The Sun Is Gone	36
Walking Home	37
5am on New Year's Eve	38
"You" I Say, and Don't Say	39
A Million Dark Possibilities	41
Now	42
Directions to Tomorrow,	43
Maybe Tomorrow	44
Raised to Believe	45
How Quickly Light is Spent	46
She's Been Trying To Tell You	47
The Gathering	48
The Big Show	49
The Trees Are All Happy Here	50
Something Wonderful Is On Its Way	51
Halfsiders	52
I Just Need Something.	53
One Finch Singing	54
Back Then	55
At the Edge of Day,	57
The Cancer Center	58
Of Those We Knew	58

Part Two: What I Mean When I Say I Love You **60**

What Worlds Have I To Give To You 61

You Smile 62

That Invisible Cord 63

This Sweet and Feral God 64

We Did Not Fall 65

You Saw My Soul First 66

You Liquefy Me 67

I Want Ten Acres In The Country 68

Things You Don't Know 69

If you're ready to love me, come 70

Forgive me 71

On a path to the end of the world 72

Part Three: Pebbles **74**

Frost Claws At My Window 75

Moment Of Silence 76

Bark Of Thunder 77

The Decisive Moment 78

Snowdrops In Memorial Park, ... 79

Steam Kisses 80

On The River 81

Plucking Blurred Stars 82

On A Child's Breath, ... 83

Baked And Dusted Day 84

The Weary World Sighs 85

Yellow Hearts 86

Feather Of A Breeze	87
Gold Leaf Slips Slowly	88
This Damp Stone,	89
Foggy Morning;	90
Unopened Presents	91
Snowflakes	92
Street Corner Nightlight	93
ACKNOWLEDGMENT	**94**

Part One:

The Perseverance of Beauty

OH, SO THAT'S POETRY

You know the one,

the one everyone says is so good,

the one who professes he from da hood,

hoping one day he'll be a professor,

product and part of the incestuous Poetry-Industrial Complex,

already so clever, he must check as he speaks,

- *you know what I'm sayin'?*

But he writes right; all meaning and no feeling.

Another joke in the echo chamber,

he never mentions Shakespeare's MFA,

or that his own will never make him

Chaucer or Milton, or even good,

but maybe just good enough

to get paid

to reach like minds,

teach tight lines

and never so much as touch a heart,

or bring a lost soul to the goddess of the arts.

Instead, he spends his days creatively committing suicide,

and his nights reading the day's suicide note

to an adoring but bewildered audience,

then beams, bows,

dances to the whistling of swans

who spend their mornings plucking petals

in search of flowers,

and their afternoons fluffing their feathers,

while you and I scratch our heads

and study the floor,

tugging at our once blue collars

now black with sweat.

"Oh, so that's poetry."

SPELLBOUND

As much as anyone else,

I enjoy the white, yellow, and pink

flutters of fairies

hovering against blue or gray,

kissing the awakening landscape

into a Monet painting,

no doubt aglow with pride,

only satisfied when we gasp and stare,

stupefied,

but it's the translucent vulnerability of a young leaf,

backlit by the gold of the morning sun,

that stops me every time,

and leaves me speechless, spellbound,

and so damn grateful.

WE DON'T DIE HERE

We don't die here.

We simply disappear;

sometimes an abrupt vanishing act,

sometimes a slow and silent fading.

One day, someone realizes they can't remember

the last time they saw someone,

and someone else says

they died.

Everyone accepts this quietly with lowered heads

because people really used to die,

and were actually seen

dead,

so we assume people still die,

but around here,

no one is ever seen

dead

except on screen.

THE MORNING CALLER

That morning in my garden,

when the angel stepped out of the fog,

I pretended I did not see him.

My brain clawed at the walls of understanding,

desperate for an explanation,

my blood so cold, my muscles froze.

When he spoke,

I heard his voice in my head

like warm caramel or liquid gold:

"I am not here for you.

I am here for the symphony

of birdsong and your heartbeat."

When he finally left, wearing the fog as a cloak,

I exhaled, and could not tell how much time had passed,

and the world snapped back into place,

with the birds singing

just a little sweeter.

FOG

Fog dissolves reality,
makes of the world a gift for me,
softly consuming all of space
but the fragment before my face,
and muffling the march of time,
catches my breath and soothes my mind
until I can't tell dream from day,
then fog invites my soul to play.

BRUSH OFF THE FROWN

Brush off the frown and smooth the rippled brow.

That which is not shall not be our master.

This is all there is; all we have is now.

All we have now is all we have allowed,

our beliefs building dreams or disasters.

Brush off the frown and smooth the rippled brow.

Know nothing now and raise no sacred cows.

No thought stops the clock or moves it faster.

This is all there is; all we have is now.

Practicing the One Art teaches us how

to look beyond matter for what matters.

Brush off the frown and smooth the rippled brow.

How many billion paths lead to the tao?

And yet not one will get you there faster.

This is all there is; all we have is now.

To thyself be true and you'll break no vow.

In one breath, no man can serve two masters.

Brush off the frown and smooth the rippled brow.

This is all there is; all we have is now.

THE PETITE FRENCH COUNTRY

The accent table beneath the window in the foyer

does not exist to bear the burden of keys

or a bowl of hard candy.

It is not there to elevate a vase

of yellow tulips, red roses, or orange dahlias.

It is there but to bare its natural beauty,

to share the luscious luminosity of its honey patina,

ever offering in exquisite elegance,

a warm whispered welcome

home.

THEY NEVER KNOW YOU AT ALL

They are always so preoccupied

with the color and texture of your bark,

the shape and shade of your leaves.

Then they want to know your name,

as if that tells them who you are.

They love to measure you soil to crown,

as if that's all there is to you.

But then they dig up your roots,

as if that tells them how high you can go.

They judge you

by which side of what mountain or river you stand on,

and determine your worth

by their need for your gift,

and how many times you have returned leaves to the earth.

And then they leave,

satisfied with their pockets full of trivia,

knowing so many little things

and so little,

they never know you at all.

LEFT

Shockangerconfusiondenialguiltrejectionbargainingdepression

lost, drowning

in fog

but what could we have done?

we simply could not hear

another's deafening cries for help

over our own

THIS IS THE MOMENT

This is the moment you ignore everyday

in favor of the ritual of distractions you call your life,

pretending you will never die

if you never truly live,

but this is neither fraction nor fragment.

This is all you'll ever have.

This is an unplanned but overdue meeting with your Self,

the you you cross the street to avoid

even in dreams,

yet run to when there's a glitch in the illusion;

the you whose hand you reach for in the dark;

the you brave enough to be here

every minute of every day,

and find in each, a glimpse of the sacred;

the you strong enough to love —

to really love! —

remaining honest and flawed and vulnerable,

willing to greet each day as a child

and be grateful

for whatever it drops at your feet.

PROUDLY EVERYTHING

Once, we were the few,

fearless pioneers

who faced and conquered the unknown

to lead an aging world

into a bright and ever-expanding future.

Now, we are many

and no one,

the new gelatinous bourgeoisie,

content and slumberous

with neither passion nor purpose.

Free to be anything,

we stand for nothing,

proudly everything

our ancestors raged against.

THE SAME HOUSE ON FIRE

While you sleep away morning in a cheap motel,

exhausted from outrunning your past,

I will go back and wait for you

among the trees at the end of the driveway

when, at eighteen, you finally fled,

escaping the hell that should have been your haven,

running blind into that pivotal Saturday night,

your tender heart racing ahead,

less fearful of the unknown, and even the unknowable,

than of that familiar and certain danger.

I will stop you long enough to tell you these truths:

none of it was your fault.

And none of it was theirs.

They simply could not give what they had never received.

He, no less lost than he had ever been,

could never be a hero, or even a better man,

and she, even with all her love and strength,

could not save you,

just as you, years later,

could not save her.

I will tell you

the savior who would find you that night

was just the same demon

in ripped jeans, with long hair,

and cool anger.

I will tell you

you were running through a different door

into the same house

on fire,

and you would call it home

until the day you could look in the mirror

and say "I love you."

But I will not tell you

that decades later and a year from now,

when you no longer see the scars,

you will run through the longest night,

into the same house

still on fire,

and you will be happy

to call it home again.

And I will not tell you

that later still,

having failed to save you,

I would sit again on the cool grass

of a pivotal Saturday night,

and tell the same truths

to your daughter.

WE ARE THE UNBLINKING EYES

We are the unblinking eyes

staring indifferently

as the world turns

ground... trees... sky...

ground, trees, sky,

groundtreessk

THE DIFFERENCE

I delight in this when it is sweet,

am grateful even when it is bitter,

and know the difference

does not exist.

I see everything in myself

and my Self in every thing,

and know the difference

does not exist.

I respect you as another

and love you as myself,

and know the difference

does not exist.

SOME WILL HATE YOU

Some will hate you.

You must know that.

They will not tell you it is because your body is

too light, too dark, too narrow, too wide, too young, too old.

They will not tell you it is because of

your name, your income, your preferences, your beliefs.

They will not tell you it is because of

their conditioning, insecurities, ignorance, ego.

They will not tell you it is because of

what you had to do to survive an experience they never had.

Some will hate you

and you must know that

even when they smile and call you friend.

Some will hate you

and you must know that

there is nothing you can do about it.

Some will hate you

and you must know that

there is nothing they will do about it.

2020 VISION

We were the ones corralled,

locked away for the unspeakable atrocities

of our unscrupulous overlords,

our only crime, believing

we were free.

Now, blinking in the sun, some see

*we are all in*habitants of *this* illusion,

trapped *together.*

THE FLEDGLINGS

As vulnerable as red pandas,

they teeter on the edge of independence.

Mimicking those who got there before them,

they quickly learn to guard themselves,

some in leather and swagger,

others in angst or anger,

but always in black.

From the comfort of the crowd,

they declare their individuality,

happy to be anything but alone

in this precarious life.

ALL I HAD TO LOSE

When you are able to speak again, tell me
which of my words upset you so?

Was it the bare facts,
honesty without emergency exits?

Was it my insistence on playing a supporting role
in my own version of events?

When you stopped seeing stars,
did you search frantically for the moment you handed me the weapon?

Did you wonder when or how I slipped from beneath your thumb?
Or have you realized I never really was?

Did you hear yourself tell me you own me,
and that there was no way out?

Remember how pleased you were with yourself
when you left me with nothing?

It was all I had to lose.

DOWNHILL FROM EVERYWHERE

Now we are all arbiters of truth.

This is the new world's religion,

with as many gods as victims,

brandishing neither cross nor flame.

Everyone is anointed.

Poisoned by the lies on our plates and our screens,

fat on our ignorance,

we lick our lips and fingers,

blessed with all we could ever want,

and all we ever want is more.

WHATEVER HAPPENS OR DOESN'T HAPPEN

Whatever happens or doesn't happen today,

be grateful

and remember one of them

could have been you.

Your name could have been pulled from his hat.

You could have been among the number

whose number was up that day,

and you would not have been saved

by the numbers or names

in your wallet,

in your closet,

in your driveway,

or even in your address.

You would not have been saved

by the color of your skin

or the colors on it;

the color of your state,

or the color of your hair that month.

You would not have been saved

by the person you sleep with,

the person you want

to be,

the person you're afraid of

being,

the person you're so sick and tired of

pretending you are.

Whatever happens or doesn't happen today,

be grateful

and remember one of the names

on the many walls like dominoes across this country

could have been yours.

IN THE MOON'S PLATINUM GLOW

In morning's golden light,

I swat the fly

and suffer,

in the moon's platinum glow,

the spider's bite.

LIFE AFTER LIFE

I brought this upon myself,

the infatuated god whose heart would not be denied,

now condemned to feel and give and never receive love,

Exiled on this rock in the river of time,

forever trying to save you,

my defiant and self-destructive immortal beloved.

Life after life, I find you.

Life after life, I love you,

knowing I cannot save you,

just as I could not when you were your mother,

and will not when your daughter becomes you.

DIGGING FOR PLUMP BEETLE BABIES

How many times must I call, cry

in love and in anger,

down these endless corridors of barren fig trees,

begging you to come back home?

The house is warm and filled

with family and friends,

with food and wine,

with light and love.

Still, you remain here,

on your knees

in the muddy shadows of twilight,

digging for plump beetle babies.

IN A HAMMERED RED ADMIRAL'S DREAM

In a hammered red admiral's dream,

characters believe they are real,

act as though they are immortal.

They create gods and time,

rituals, traditions, fairy tales,

differences, hope, pain, and consequences.

They imagine cause and purpose,

love and freedom,

things to kill

and die for,

anything

to add the illusion of depth and duration

to their congenital delusion

in the surreal hallucination

of a drunk butterfly.

THE PLEA

Dear distant and baneful knaves,

pretending to be kings and gods,

feasting on your well-fed slaves,

have mercy on me, overlords,

and grant me please this damp cold cave,

where exiled 'til death we'll be

content and very well-behaved,

silence, solitude, and me.

THE GIANTS ARE AFRAID

I think the big people are afraid

of the giants they want to be.

I think they must have daydreams and nightmares about the giants,

about being in a parade of giants,

and about growing up,

and about not growing up,

and I think the giants are afraid

of the dark, and of the gods

they pretend to be.

And I think they have nightmares too

about falling,

and about dying

just like us.

I KEEP FORGETTING

I am not Jesus;

I keep forgetting I am

and am not human.

I keep forgetting to be

whole and happy,

here, now,

to dance in the euphoria

between miracle and misery.

I keep forgetting to be

everyone, every thing;

to not be the wave, wavering,

pure potential, pausing.

I keep forgetting to jump;

to not hesitate

on the threshold of every possible heaven.

THE SUN IS GONE

The sun is gone. It has burned out.
The world is black and cold.
The sky hangs low, heavy with doubt,
and grief has made me old.

Mourning keeps Morpheus at bay.
Sorrow slaughtered the sheep,
and I would gladly trade my days
for rest peaceful and deep.

But still, days come and come again,
each but a winter's night.
My aching soul has said "amen",
but cannot see the light.

WALKING HOME

I want so much to sit with you,

to hold you, absorb your pain,

and show you

we are both the light

and the shadows on the wall.

I want to tell you

we are all humming the same song,

walking home

together, alone

in the dark.

5 AM ON NEW YEAR'S EVE

I turn on the bright, cold light
to find a healthy brown slug
exploring the smooth white landscape
of my toilet.

Startled, disgusted, and confused,
I look around
for others and an entry point
while the sleek intruder moves along.

I wonder if she or he is excited or terrified,
as lost and curious as I,
safe for the moment, but uncertain
in this beautiful alien terrain,
trying to find a way back home.

"YOU" I SAY, AND DON'T SAY

You ask me what I would try to save

if the house was on fire.

"You" I say,

and don't say

I would rush you to the door,

push you outside,

tell you to run,

and I would lock the door behind you.

I don't tell you I would seek out the most comfortable place

to sit or lie, waiting

to be kissed, embraced, consumed

by the beautiful, ravenous flames.

I don't tell you I would worry about what I was wearing,

perhaps even hastily change my clothes

so that only natural fibers would be found

among my reclined remains.

I don't tell you because I saw you

years later,

sobbing on an expensive sofa

with an even more expensive view,

telling a very expensive ear

what your mother said to you

one rainy spring afternoon

when you were eight, and bored,

just trying to make small talk.

A MILLION DARK POSSIBILITIES

She laughs at the man who wakes early to work hard

just as his father did,

while she gets money from the state every month,

and lives rent free.

Low income, she says, smiling knowingly,

but minimal effort too.

All day long, she sings,

as free as her mother was,

and just as her mother did,

she takes her daughter dancing

to the 24-hour convenience store

in small black hours,

ignorant of, or undaunted by

a million dark possibilities.

NOW

Life is not at all as we had planned now;
not a single moment goes unscanned now.

Victims of all we can't understand now,
no one's more a woman or a man now.

Look 'round: there's no one to hold our hands now
as our connected lives go unmanned now.

We've done to the earth all it can stand now;
we're all alone on alien land now.

You and I are one and not human now.
Everything is exactly as planned now.

DIRECTIONS TO TOMORROW

Tell me then, how the sun rises,

give me directions to tomorrow.

Show me all of God's disguises,

and an hour I may borrow.

Tell me now just how long life is

so I'll know when to start living,

and how much love the human heart fits,

so I'll know when to stop giving.

Show me what next Thursday looks like,

and all the code that's so clever,

and when we lie beneath the stars,

don't be shy; show me forever.

MAYBE TOMORROW

This is where your heart has led you;

to a bed of pine needles,

with moss for a pillow,

and a blanket of stars.

Hear the river rushing by,

the wind tickling the trees,

and hearts of every size playing their part

in the same symphony as yours.

Maybe tomorrow

you will feel the sun

kiss the feathers of your wings.

RAISED TO BELIEVE

Here, we accept what we're told
is acceptable.

Here, we celebrate
being celebrated for who we're not.

Here, the weak and the wounded hide
in the comfort and pleasures of the familiar.

Here, everyone's a victim, and everyone's okay
and everything is not.

Here, we are kept addicted and distracted,
oblivious stars of the shit show.

Here, we are the cheapest resource
with the highest profit margin.

Here, everything is made up,
made truth, made law.

Here, every vote, every dollar, and no one matters.
Here, we're raised to believe.

HOW QUICKLY LIGHT IS SPENT

Did I, from nothing, not just toddle among the Tulips,

grasping hands large enough to carry the world?

Oh, was it not just noon?

How quickly light is spent;

now there's gold in the sky and at my feet

with this morning's nestlings flying south!

Too soon, too soon the dragon comes,

but I will face him without regrets,

for I did indeed drink to the lees,

and have earned that long and dreamless sleep.

SHE'S BEEN TRYING TO TELL YOU

She's been trying to tell you
you're not the self-contained sensory apparatus you think you are.

She's been trying to tell you
the sun didn't rise this morning …or ever.

She's been trying to tell you
time is a game of Peek-A-Boo you never stopped playing.

She's been trying to tell you
you missed the end of the world. Again.

But you're too busy being busy,
addicted to distraction.

Maybe next time the sky goes black with crows,
you'll pay attention,

listen. And hear
all she's been trying to tell you.

THE GATHERING

I know what you mean though,
it's been sunny and dry all week.

By the way, I must tell you
that dress is absolutely gorgeous,
and I love your necklace!

Should we go to the other side now?
There's less smoke over there.
We can freshen up our drinks
and sit in the shade of that old Yew.
Besides, the smell of coolant mixed with gasoline
is so strong here.

I think there's more blood on that side too,
and I haven't seen the body yet; have you?

THE BIG SHOW

Come one as all to the only show in town!
This show's been running since the day of your birth.
Guaranteed the greatest illusion around!

You'll lose everything but get your money's worth.
So many wonders! Do not believe your eyes.
You are the star of the Greatest Show on Earth!

The person beside you is you in disguise!
Pull back the curtain! The universe is there!
All your dreams can come true just as advertised.

What you believe is what you'll find everywhere.
Don't mind your mind and the truth will be revealed,
so come! Step right up! Step right up if you dare!

Create your reality, that is the deal.
There's nothing to fear because no thing is real!

THE TREES ARE ALL HAPPY HERE

The trees are all happy here,

with everything they need

and no predators but time and man.

They are so happy in fact,

that they often spontaneously break

into synchronized dance,

apparently to wind-songs

we are too civilized to hear.

And oh, how beautifully they dance,

gorgeous, glorious, graceful

in their luxurious shades of green.

And every time the trees dance,

wherever I am,

my soul flies off to join them,

singing, laughing, twirling,

drunk on joy,

and homesick,

as it flitters and flutters

from treetop to treetop.

SOMETHING WONDERFUL IS ON ITS WAY

Something wonderful is on its way.

It may be small, but don't dismiss it.

Don't be so quick to turn away;

very few blessings are explicit.

It may be small, but don't dismiss it;

miracles hide among the mundane.

Very few blessings are explicit,

and the mind of man today, profane.

Miracles hide among the mundane,

treasures for the heart that still believes.

The mind of man today is profane.

Be grateful and ready to receive

treasures for the heart that still believes,

always filled with love and ne'er dismayed.

Be grateful and ready to receive;

something wonderful is on its way.

HALFSIDERS

Halfsiders,

the fledglings neither flew nor fell,

but perched in cloud castles,

knowing neither sun nor soil,

nor moonlight on their wings,

and never heard a true heart's chirp,

or knew what song to sing.

I JUST NEED SOMETHING

I need water, yeast, hops, barley.

I need sugar, fat, preservatives, artificial colors and flavors.

I need grapes, potassium sorbate, calcium carbonate, sulfites.

I need ammonia, nicotine, formaldehyde, lead, arsenic.

I need attention, approval, affection, distraction.

I need dopamine. I need the blue pill.

I need THC. I need caffeine.

I need something.

I just need

something

ONE FINCH SINGING

I know you

don't know you

are the bark beetle in Eden.

I know you

don't know you

are the rust on the chain.

Go on singing yourself,

celebrating yourself

to the edge

and over

into the dust of time.

One morning, the earth will awaken

to the sound of one finch singing,

your monument,

a layer of plastic in a rock.

BACK THEN

Back then,

he was a shadow

downtown

and a ghost

uptown,

and everywhere,

a known yet unknown ever-present threat,

threatened,

a monster captured, confined to a box

in a box

in a box,

made to feel he shouldn't exist,

wish he didn't,

and called every thing

but the child of the god who gave us

blues,

peanut butter,

jazz,

potato chips,

Motown,

hip hop,

cool,

so many delicacies in the American soul's feast,

so many irreplaceable threads

in the fabric of the American experience.

But that was then…

AT THE EDGE OF DAY

At the edge of day,

on the threshold of solace,

comes the furtive haunting,

the whisper of water,

the caress of a breeze,

the sweet soft scent of soil.

Somewhere deep but rising,

you know it's you

calling yourself back home.

THE CANCER CENTER

Not by any sense but a shiver of the heart,

we always know when Kalma is here, watching, waiting,

Surma at her side.

We do not wonder for whom they have come;

their client is always aware

of that appointment.

When they leave, snug in the client's shadow,

we bow our heads,

our hearts filled with Chrysanthemums,

and take no pleasure

in their silent suffering

as they move through the lobby,

always warm with love

and defiantly bright

with hope.

OF THOSE WE KNEW

Day after day they come,

arising at dawn, solar-powered reproductions

of those we knew

yesterday,

so subtly different, we never notice.

We interact with them, then watch them advance,

moving past us with the sun,

disappearing in the dark.

Tomorrow, new ones will come,

just like us,

so subtly different, we never notice.

Part Two:

What I Mean

When I Say I Love You

WHAT WORLDS HAVE I TO GIVE TO YOU

What worlds have I to give to you
but those within my mind and heart,
which I would give if they would do,
that you and I would never part.

That you and I would never part,
I'd turn my back on other dreams.
A whole life for a crumbled tart
would laugh those blind to all I've seen.

They'd laugh, those blind to all I've seen,
who'll never know your worth and ways,
or just how blessed indeed I'd be
to worship you throughout my days.

And though my love would never do,
still, until death, I love you true.

YOU SMILE

You smile

and some days,
it takes hours

to fit back
into my small life

and sometimes,
it takes days

to patch the cracks
that let hope in.

THAT INVISIBLE CORD

Afterward, we walked lightly,

holding hands,

smiling in the gold dust

of the afternoon sun,

bound by that invisible cord,

so fragile, it could be broken

by the breath of a white lie,

yet so strong,

it could keep the world at bay

forever.

THIS SWEET AND FERAL GOD

but how are we to ever know,

to sense or even dare imagine,

the height and depth and breadth of it,

the power and ferocity

of love,

this sweet and feral god

for whom we must all become martyrs?

WE DID NOT FALL

We did not fall;

we walked into this.

Blind,

and drunk on dreams and desperation,

we walked into this.

Now, from the outside, our friends barely see us.

To them, we are always on the horizon,

forever fading, but never gone.

Inside, there is us

and the one thing everything has collapsed into,

even time,

tock-ticking,

first flying, then falling in on itself,

clock sticking, then

starting over,

halfway through the same hour.

When we resurface, we will be strangers to even ourselves,

each telling a very different version

of the same tragedy.

YOU SAW MY SOUL FIRST

You saw my soul first, as none before you.
Your smile enjoined my heart to adore you.

Oh, but when hope is the thing with talons,
what could my deeply scarred heart feel for you?

War-weary, my cool head dared take a stand,
commanding my weak heart to ignore you.

For so long, how valiantly I fought,
'til on my knees in dreams, I implored you.

Do not smile. Give me no reason to pine,
or I'm yours until death, I assure you!

YOU LIQUEFY ME

You liquefy me.

You smile,

and I pour out of myself

to fall at your feet,

intent on being absorbed,

hell-bent on being part of you.

If not for this, why

do I exist?

I must be in your blood,

necessary for your existence,

and someday, in tears of joy,

flowing past your smile,

to evaporate

into the air you breathe.

I WANT TEN ACRES IN THE COUNTRY

I want ten acres in the country humans can't see,

with a creek to sing me lullabies,

wildflowers to entice me,

a mountain to watch over me,

and you

to hold every day

in the doorway of a dream,

and show you

that love can be synonymous with worship.

THINGS YOU DON'T KNOW

but you don't know

you don't know

what love is,

that love is

what we're made of,

why the heart is the first human organ.

You don't know

even in the dark,

you can't see the light

if you're looking

in the wrong direction.

You don't even know

you walk a hundred miles every night

in your dreams,

always searching, not for your soul's mate,

but for yourself.

IF YOU'RE READY TO LOVE ME, COME

If you're ready to love me, come.

Come to me wearing the bright silence of dreams,

with only dew or honey on your lips,

and no talk of the world.

Come, and whisper without words

of a place without us

in a dimension we can't even imagine.

Come, touch me

where no one can see,

and we will be forever, not in love,

or even lovers, but love itself.

Only when you're ready to surrender,

to abandon all you are for all we can be,

come.

FORGIVE ME

Forgive me.

I will not pretend to be anything.

I am a lamb on its first sunny morning

after being born on a stormy night.

I am delirious,

on my knees before you, your wings wide, welcoming.

Fevered, drunk on anticipation, I cannot be cool.

Forgive me; I prayed but dared not believe

dreams sometimes come true.

ON A PATH TO THE END OF THE WORLD

My entire body aches

to experience your entire body.

My eyes burn

to see yours blaze

on the edge of ecstasy.

My fingers twitch

anticipating

the warm silk of your hidden skin.

My lips quiver,

longing to know yours,

time and again,

sucking every drop of honey from the comb.

My hands shake,

yearning to liberate your glory,

but slowly, slowly

as if I am moving in a dream

between tulips,

kissing every dew-wet petal

while you float, heels over head

on a path to the end of the world.

My tongue is so sore

from being bitten.

I must love you.

I must explore your exquisite landscape

until I am dizzy with desire,

setting the universe on fire

and letting the whole damn thing burn

while I give you pleasure after pleasure,

each of us dying countless little deaths

until we wash up on the shore of morning.

Part Three:
Pebbles

frost claws at my window

wind shreds the night.

Soaked, my pillow is colder still.

moment of silence…

antique crystal vase

now a field of jagged jewels

bark of thunder

beyond the rain-streaked car window

red and blue stars

the decisive moment –

my shadow leans forward

as I look back.

Snowdrops in Memorial Park,

the Yew, the dew, and the fallen

Oak leaves and acorns

steam kisses

the frosted kitchen window;

the first spoonful of porridge

on the river

that once ran red,

cherry blossoms, paper boats

plucking blurred stars

from the ceiling,

the taste of salt.

on a child's breath,

one hundred fairies

leave home

baked and dusted day

a child's hand stops the car –

lemonade!

the weary world sighs

the giant weeps

gold into the stream

yellow hearts

on the forest floor;

the creek whispers

feather of a breeze –

Ginkgo blows canary kisses

into the cool twilight

gold leaf slips slowly

through silver moonlight

soundlessly

to sleep

this damp stone,

and this damp stone;

on this damp stone,

a yellow leaf

foggy morning;

into my steaming cup

another tear

unopened presents –

no fire can warm our first Christmas

without you

snowflakes

same tongue

different person

street corner nightlight

the town sleeps

under a down comforter

ACKNOWLEDGMENT

My deep appreciation to my brave and generous friends who gave their time and attention to read early versions of the poems in this book and provide feedback which helped to make this collection significantly better than it would have otherwise been. I am eternally grateful.

U
N
I
R
1

Live compassionately;
love always.

www.ingramcontent.com/pod-product-compliance
Lightning Source LLC
Chambersburg PA
CBHW060846050426
42453CB00008B/850